Our Golden Seasons

Kathy Bird

Gaye,
Hooray for
seniors and
those who love
them.
Love,
Bird

Our Golden Seasons

roots of resilience

old scars from healed wounds

mature and majestic

standing straight and tall

reach for the light

branch out

arms raised to the heavens holding joy

billows bright with color against a sky of brilliant blue

possibilities boundless and bursting

the autumns of aging filled to the brim

with light, love, and laughter

of living

Our Golden Seasons

About the Book

I have a great talent for procrastination. Being busy, eating out, spending time with friends and family, travel, exercising, computer games, watching series and basketball on TV, and even errands took precedent over writing another book. Thoughts of funny experiences in senior life, some ideas for a senior dictionary, and memories of inspiring stories from seniors sat in the back of my mind. They were patiently waiting to get a word in edgewise. For years, the procrastination noise was deafening and more powerful.

In March of 2020 the pandemic hit, the world stopped, and everything changed. In April, I turned seventy and was deemed by the media to be vulnerable and elderly. Shelter-in-place dictates successfully blocked many of my procrastination avenues. Computer games and watching series on TV were getting old. Since cooking, sewing, and heavy cleaning were not options, my only alternative was to write another book. After all, someone had to speak for the "vulnerable" older set. Our Golden Seasons, a book for and about seniors, was born.

Gleaning hope and inspiration from others has helped me navigate seniordom. Using the telephone and in-person social distancing, I interviewed strong seniors who had amazing stories to tell. Each senior story, although perfectly capable of standing alone, joined with the other narratives to present a bigger and more complete picture of the art of growing old. Colorful threads are woven throughout the stories, tying them together into a stunning senior tapestry of strength and beauty. As it turned out, each person chose a number of tools in order to best deal with their unique challenges. Some wished to have names changed, but all gave me permission to write their story. For those seniors who are now deceased, I received feedback and approval from family members.

Since aging is like riding waves of uncharted experiences, humor has helped me stay afloat. The senior dictionary, funny family stories, and laughing at aggravating aging situations may offer a lighthearted look at growing old. Hopefully, this book will provide some perspective, entertainment, humor, and inspiration.

In the end, writing a book was much more fun and fulfilling than pandemic procrastination. I am glad, however, that life is pretty much back to normal.

Table of Contents

1
The Age of Acceptance!?!

In March of 2020, the COVID-19 task force began their
briefings. I learned fairly quickly that I fit the criterion of a senior
and was included in the "most vulnerable among us." Day after
day, I was reminded of my age. I will agree, the information was
important, but frankly the message was getting a little old. In April,
I turned seventy, and the message from then on grew extremely old.
A senior in March and elderly in April? I don't think so! Whoever
heard of an elderly baby boomer?

Through my twenties, thirties, and early forties, I chose to
identify with the category of "young adult." I was resistant to the
designation "middle aged." This resistance rose to my consciousness
at the age of forty-two while driving my twelve-year-old son,
Sean, down a steep, winding dirt road. If my memory serves me,
I was clutching the steering wheel. Often my memory servings
are equivalent to a sugar-laden dessert filled with the sweet empty
calories of unhealthy denial. This particular memory, however,
had a bitter taste of reality. As I said, my wet, sweaty hands were
clutching the steering wheel. The hands were supposed to be at
ten and two but had slipped to nine and three as salty beads of
moisture dripped down my forehead, blurring my vision. I was

trying to stay calm in the midst of the latest heat wave of hot flashes. I assume twelve-year-old Sean, assessing the situation (steep inclines, no guard rails, slippery steering wheel, dripping mom) stated his truth.

"Mom, if we get in an accident, I think I should be the one to live. After all, I am in my growth cycle. You are almost out of your reproductive cycle and heading into your death cycle."

Slowing down to a crawl, I responded, "I will be careful so we both live." This seemed to satisfy Sean, and he nodded in agreement. Not me… inside I was hot, both physically and mentally. "No way am I close to my death cycle, I'm not even middle aged!" I clung to "young adult" status throughout my forties. I slowly and begrudgingly succumbed to middle age in my fifties.

When I turned sixty-five, I noted that the US government, the airlines, AAA, and many restaurants deemed me to be a senior. Doing the math, if I were truly still middle-aged at sixty-five, I would live to 130. To cling to this belief would have been delusional. Reason took over, and I graciously accepted the senior discount and designation. Did I say graciously?

Looking youngish in my alleged "death cycle" was not easy, especially with my "middle-age" mentality. Through the years, there were people in my life suggesting ways, subtle and not-so-subtle, to maintain a sense of young-ishness. Hairdressers highlighted my problem of grayness. When that no longer worked, they used dye to get to the roots of the issue.

My friend, Stacey, informed me coloring the hair wasn't enough—beautiful hands were a must. Thus started the fake-nail manicure.

Face wrinkles galore required a day and night three-step skin regimen and a twelve-step make-up process. Since this eighteen-step daily chore turned out to be a weak cover story, another friend suggested jewelry. Jewelry was supposed to add color and beauty to my appearance, all the while taking attention away from my face. Wow, what a lot of work to appear young-ish!

Now I am seventy, and according to the coronavirus task force I am elderly and vulnerable. Due to the shut-down because of COVID-19, my nails are suffering from an attachment disorder. The color is leaving my hair, and I will soon find out whether my gray is silvery or mousy. My wrinkles, feeling free, have come out of hiding. They are happily proliferating as my face and make up process has dwindled to four steps from the eighteen-step process it had been facing. In public, my face appropriately and safely hides behind a mask.

Yes, I am seventy. Now, not using my youngish-appearance

aids, I am looking my age. I am a senior baby boomer who has the freedom and determination to reject the term elderly. The coronavirus has reminded me that life is precious. I am gratefully gray. I am so thankful for the freedom I enjoy living in this fabulous country. I am blessed to be retired in a beautiful shelter in place even though I am forced to cook. I am eternally thankful to my family, friends, and all Americans who are making sacrifices and dramatically adjusting their lifestyle so we seniors can continue to enjoy our life (not death) cycle.

2
Tools for Aging

If I were to write down our life's journey in words, I picture a book consisting of five parts. Within each part would be numerous chapters.

Part I - Childhood

A romp through the years with boundless energy. Purpose: to learn and grow.

Part II - Adolescence

Pushing through the years with a resistant, sullen, opinionated posture. Purpose: to separate from parents and develop identity and roles.

Part III - Adult

Running through the years while juggling work, relationships, and family. Purpose: to establish intimacy and relationships with others.

Part IV - Middle Age

These are speed-walking years of incorporating work, family, and community into life. Purpose: contribute to society and be a part of a family.

Part V - Senior!

A casual stroll through life's garden, pausing to notice beauty using all five senses. Purpose: assess and make sense of life and its meaning. Presently, my purpose is to write a book for and about seniors.

We have arrived at our age with many tools! How wonderful that we are able to continue our story, through our golden seasons, to the very end. Let's take a look at life's last:

C - courage/creativity/choice
H - humor/heart
A - attitude/acceptance/adaptable
P - perspective/priorities
T - trust/thankfulness
E - experience/empathy
R - resiliency/rituals/reminiscing
S - spirit/sharing

With all these natural and learned traits, no wonder we have seniority! These tools are liberally sprinkled throughout the following stories. Each senior used multiple resources, listed and unlisted, to successfully survive life's storms in order to thrive.

We also have many aids and appliances in addition to these tools to help with the journey though the aging process.

AAA - Aids and Appliances for Aging

BiPAP, CPAP, EKG and CT
Chiropractic, massage, surgery and PT

Procedures, screenings, ice and heat packs for pains
Braces, crutches, orthotics, walkers and canes

Hair dye, fake nails, bralettes and lotions
Pills, pill boxes, prescriptions and potions

Hearing aids, CC, reading glasses and large prints
Water piks, toothbrushes, dentures and mouth splints

Exercise equipment, walking sticks and humidified air
Neck pillows, remotes, adjustable bed and chair

Some aids and appliances listed on this page
May make life easier for those of our age.

3
Early-Aged Terms of Endearment

The name calling started when I, Kathy Bird, and he, Steve Yocum, began dating. Since Kathy and Steve are prevalent and boring names from the fifties, we spiced up our relationship early on by calling each other Bird and Yokes (yolks).

I added two early-Bird appliances to my life before becoming a senior simply because I was in love. In my early forties, my semi-sweet husband-to-be strongly suggested I get hearing aids.

"Bird, if you would like me to watch TV with you, you will need to get hearing aids," Yokes announced early in our relationship. He explained he couldn't handle the extremes of the sound blowing out his eardrums vs. my constant "What did they say?" question at a reasonable volume. My heart and head heard him, and I bought bilateral aids. I love being able to hear! One of my relationship issues was solved. This appliance definitely aided my career as psychotherapist and gave new meaning to the phrase "active listening." Now, as a senior, I use both closed captions (CC) and hearing aids when watching TV with my husband.

Months after I made the sound decision to buy hearing aids, and a month before my marriage, Yokes and I went backpacking. Hiking out, my feet, knees and hips hurt so much, I could barely walk. He ended up shouldering both packs for the last mile. "Bird, if you want me to go backpacking with you again…" At this point in our relationship, I knew what was coming.

"I know, I know, you want me to get my feet fixed." The following week, I visited a podiatrist. The M.D., after studying my feet for a long time, looked up at me with a concerned, let-her-down-easy doctor expression and said, "At your age—" (not even middle-aged) "—sometimes body parts get worn out. If you were a car (a car?), I would say your tires are out of round." Still smarting from the "at your age" comment, I begrudgingly accepted the analogy he was trying to drive home. After all, walking is a most rudimentary form of transportation, and I wanted to walk with the least amount of pain. Now, I depend on orthotics and have for years.

4
Later Tools, Aids and Appliances

~~~

Staying Abreast

In my sixties, I ventured into a bra store with my sister-in-law, who is seven years older. After the helpful clerk fitted me with a day bra, she kindly said, "And what do you wear at night?"

Thinking this question rather personal, but wanting to be truthful and nice I said, "Nothing."

Her eyes widened, looking up to the ceiling, apparently searching for the right words, she said, "Well… um… when you sleep (at your age) with no support, the breast tissue tends to break down." She made a downward motion with her hands as her eyes looked fleetingly at my chest.

"What would you suggest?" I asked, wanting to stay abreast of the latest fashion aids.

Her eyes smiled as she grabbed and held up a piece of fabric. "This is a lounge bralette."

I looked pointedly at my sister-in-law. "Did you know about this?"

"Why, yes, we called this lounge bralette a night bra. I wear one every night and have for years."

"Why didn't you tell me?"

"The subject never came up!" she stated definitively.

"Now I know why the subject never came up," I said, glancing down at my sagging breasts. "I didn't know about lounge bralettes."

We all laughed at my problem keeping up with the times. I bought two lounge bralettes.

The Eyes Have It

I have learned as body parts grow old, it is good to have a new perspective.

I usually wear glasses because they are just easier. When giving a speech, however, I need to see both near and far at the same time, so I wear a contact in one eye. The contact corrects for my nearsightedness. My non-contact eye lets me see up close. Speech-giving is one of my least favorite activities. Just thinking about speaking in front of an audience causes major panic. One afternoon, three hours before speech time, I put my contact in. What happened next totally blindsided me. I couldn't see anything out of that eye. Losing sight of common sense, I panicked.

"Oh no, my right eye has given up! I'm going blind in one eye. I'm only sixty-four."

I immediately called my eye doctor stating frantically that

I had an emergency. Fifteen minutes later, the doctor called me back. The doctor calmly reassured me I wasn't going blind. In his perspective, the problem had nothing to do with my eye, but it had everything to do with the contact. After taking the contact out, I found the manufacturer had put two contacts on top of each other instead of one in the capsule. Talk about double vision. I had automatically blamed my age, instead of using my head. I was relieved I wasn't going blind. I was also disappointed I didn't have an excuse to cancel my speech.

About a month after the contact fiasco, I was tending to my house plants. I noticed some of the plants were swarming with little mites. I grabbed my plants and took them outside. The bugs accompanied the plants… or so I thought. Back in the house, I relaxed on the couch, looking out on our beautiful view. The view was instantly marred by a bunch of little black flying objects.

"Oh no, the bugs are back!" I yelled, while vigorously swatting the air. The swatting seemed to have little effect. Having just learned to not blame my age, it took me a while to realize the black spots weren't bugs—they were floaters in my eyes. Eyes get floaters with age. OK, now I could see that sometimes problems did have to do with my age. I would have to broaden my perspective again.

Two other aging tools now came in to play—experience and

priorities. How should I handle my two extremely embarrassing and dumb mistakes? My aged experience and wisdom tell me I make dumb mistakes, but that doesn't mean I'm dumb or a mistake. Dumb mistakes are not high on my priority list. I would rather spend my time looking past the floaters to my beautiful view. Now, since my brain has adjusted, I am able to block out my eye floaters and focus totally on the view.

Remote Learning

My husband has been dealing with back pain for years. He finally decided to have a spinal cord stimulator implanted in his back.

Anytime a surgery happens, I like to ask a lot of questions. This surgery was no exception. When I found out that Yokes had a battery, a battery charger, and a remote, my logical question for the doctor was, "If my husband gets out of line, am I able to use the remote to zap him?" The answer was yes. I had another tool in my arsenal.

About six months after the spinal stimulator surgery, I accompanied Yokes to a preop appointment for another surgery. A nurse in training was giving my husband an EKG. He was lying on the table happily breathing, but the nurse-in-training was freaking out.

The nurse came out with a high-pitched question, "Mr. Yocum, do you have a pacemaker?"

"No," Yokes calmly replied.

Following this line of questioning, my brain began spinning and landed on a mind picture of the remote.

I replied, "No, but he has a spinal cord stimulator."

"Oh," said the nurse, relieved. "Would you please turn it off so I can get it an accurate reading."

It appeared by Yokes' breathing that his heart rate had accelerated, but the monitor hadn't changed. He said apologetically, "I'm sorry, I left my remote at home."

I thought to myself, this would be a great time to zap him if I had the remote in my possession. Taking the high road, I said sweetly, "Would you like me to drive home and get the remote?" The nurse nodded vigorously, and Yokes mumbled his fourth apology. Luckily, home wasn't far from the clinic.

I arrived back at the clinic, holding the remote. Resisting the temptation to zap, I handed it to my husband. He immediately shut his stimulator down. The nurse reran the EKG with a normal result. Yay, Yokes could and would get to have another surgery! Remote learning has its place after all.

.

5

To Dementia with Love

My mother was born in 1923. For the most part, the goal of college-bound women of Mom's generation was attaining a "Mrs. degree." After marrying, the expectation was to become a homemaker extraordinaire, excelling in cooking, sewing, and housekeeping. The second responsibility for the wife of that era was to raise kids, while the husband's job was to raise the money to support the family.

Mom had no interest in the Mrs. degree. Mom's goal in college was an education, which resulted in a BA. She then went on to grad school. While getting her MA, she was hired by her sorority as a graduate counselor to set up a new chapter. The following year, she was hired by the same sorority as a field secretary, which involved traveling from college to college and chapter to chapter. In Montana, she met and later married Dad. She was twenty-six years old.

Mom had many interests: education, literature, politics, economics, current events, architecture, gardening, charitable organizations, travel, and parenting. Yes, I said parenting. I was the oldest of four. Mom loved being a mom! She thought being a stay-at-home mom was one of life's most important careers. While always very active in her community, her first priority was her children. She was, however, an unconventional mom because she thought sewing, cooking, proper place settings, or housekeeping had very little to do with good parenting.

She would cook, sew, and clean if needed, but she didn't like it. Mom would creatively cook up ways to avoid cooking whenever possible. When Dad would go out of town for business, Mom would announce it was time for a crazy dinner. Each child would pick out and prepare the food they would like to share. A typical crazy dinner might include cake batter, cookie dough, bread and gravy, and popcorn. Mom would always choose carrots for nutrition. We would all get sick and be ready for another crazy dinner the minute Dad went out of town again.

When we went on our annual summer vacation, Mom instituted the Golden Chef Award. Each member of the family would be responsible for making a dinner. We would all vote, and the yearly winner's name would be engraved on a plaque. Mom never entered the contest. Dad always entered and never won.

She was known for her rubber gravy. One time the gravy was so hard to swallow that we put it in our golden retriever's dog dish. Tash, wagging his tail, couldn't believe his good fortune. After he grabbed a big gravy glob, his tail went down, however, as he tried valiantly using his tongue to get the gravy off the roof of his mouth. This went on for many minutes. In desperation, he used a giant tongue swipe to dislodge the glob. Relieved, he spit the gravy into his dish. Mom said she saw him later bury the gravy in disgust. Since mom was the only witness, this event has not been verified. Mom thought this story hilarious. She would play-act the dog trying to get the gravy off the roof of his mouth for anyone who would listen.

Mom promoted her reputation as a terrible cook. She liked the low expectations when it came to potlucks. She did try to please her children, however. My brother asked her to get a recipe from the school cook. She did. The school cook, in her twenty years of cooking at the school, had never had a request for a recipe. The cook was quite pleased, although she had to cut the recipe down quite a bit.

Mom made it very clear she didn't like to sew. When I was a six-year-old, a button fell off of one of my favorite dresses. I started to cry. Mom asked me why I was crying. "I will have to wait a whole year for Grandma to come here and sew on this button." Mom immediately sewed on my button.

One time, I asked Mom to sew me some pantaloons. They were a disaster! The crotch was just a little above my ankles, which meant I had to walk like a penguin. I never wore the pantaloons and put them in the Goodwill bag, thinking Goodwill would probably reject them. Even Goodwill has standards.

Years later, because of money issues, we were bracing for a very sparse Christmas. On Christmas morning to our surprise, under the tree were four colorfully wrapped presents! Mom had wrapped a present for each child. Attached to each gift was a card labeled "goofs from yesteryear." In my gift box, I found my old pantaloons.

"I hated these!"

"I know," said Mom with a smile. "That's why I wrapped them up." A wonderful family Christmas was had by all. Thanks, Mom!

Mom was smart, educated, active, attentive, independent, fun, funny, and very creative. We were happy kids. Mom had very strong opinions. More important than her opinions, however, was her desire for her children to learn to think for themselves. In junior high, my history teacher gave us a book to read. After Mom perused the book, she said, "This book is one way to look at the world. After reading this one, would you be willing to read another book showing another way to view the world? Let's then discuss it." Living with Mom involved a lot more reading and a lot more learning.

She was a humorous and wise disciplinarian. When it was time for my date to go home, Mom, wearing a robe, would walk through the room, not saying anything, holding a lit candle. This was the not-so-subtle hint for my boyfriend to leave.

Why do you need all this background information about my mother? I want you to know what kind of mother I had, in order to have an idea of what I lost. Mom started changing in her late sixties. At first, I didn't notice. When I did become aware of some behavior changes, I explained them away.

Mom had suffered significant losses in her fifties and sixties. Dad lost all his money, my parents had to move out of the house they built and lived in for many years, their lifestyle drastically changed, they divorced, she lost both her parents, and her children were each going through various traumas of their own. Then, on Mom's sixty-sixth birthday, the unthinkable, the unimaginable happened. Her daughter Susan was murdered by her estranged husband. Our whole family was devastated. It took all of us many years to heal.

I thought Mom's behavior changes were a response to these losses. I just knew she would bounce back and return to the old Mom. She never did. I tried to accept the new Mom with mixed results. The new Mom suffered from short-term memory loss, would get physically and mentally lost, forget where her bank was located, and get her times and days mixed up.

All these behaviors were concerning but behaviors I could understand and accept. What I had the most trouble swallowing was the absence of her wit and positive attitude. All my life, her humor and optimism had softened and lightened harsh realities. The old Mom was forever squeezing the bitterness of life's lemons into the refreshing and exhilarating taste of lemonade. She made every crisis palatable with her special flavor of courage and resiliency. All that disappeared in the deep, dark hole of dementia. When she lost the ability to make lemonade, we were left with an unhappy, angry, bitter Mom. I had a tough time accepting the change.

In the later stages of Mom's dementia, I only had to deal with the new Mom from a distance. My sister Leslie witnessed her decline day in and day out. Even as a little girl, Leslie walked, skipped, and danced along a spiritual path. Later, together with her very kind husband Mark, they became caregivers to both of our parents at the end of their lives. I say caregivers because Leslie and Mark gave and gave and gave every day. I am so grateful!

Even with the help of her spiritual world, Leslie struggled to accept the new Mom. Leslie told me a story, illustrating her frustration and feeling of loss. It was the year 2000, and Mom was seventy-seven years old. Leslie's routine was to take Mom to the bank every week in order to help her feel more independent. Mom would withdraw exactly $60 to use for her weekly spending money. On this occasion, Mom asked the teller to give her $2000.

"Mom, why $2000?" Leslie asked. "You usually get $60."

Mom answered without hesitation, "Oh, Leslie. Y2K, of course."

I was impressed—it sounded like the old Mom. "How funny and clever of her to link the computer crisis to her bank withdrawal," I exclaimed.

The sadness in Leslie's voice was heartrending. "No, I asked Mom what she meant by her Y2K comment. She just gave me a blank stare. She had no idea why she said what she said."

What I got from Mom growing up was returned to her in old age by my children. My kids handled Mom much better than I. They sat beside their Nana with no expectations. They just simply loved and appreciated her. Mom, I think, sensed the non-judgmental support, and for brief moments the old Mom spark would return. My children were able to shower unconditional love on their Nana—the same unconditional love I received from Mom for so many years.

Dementia is devastating, but love is everlasting. I am so thankful for all the many gifts of love I have received. I love you, Mom. Thanks for everything.

6

A P.C. Perspective

My dad, Philip Cullen Bird, known as P.C. to his friends,
had a unique perspective on life. Dad encouraged all who knew
him to look at the big picture. Dad not only looked at it, he lived it.
His big picture was housed in his head. His active mind resided in
the clouds. From on high, he clearly saw the forest, often missing
the trees. His big-picture world was filled with optimism, beauty,
knowledge, excellence, dreams, challenge, perseverance, ideas,
and most of all humor.

Dad thoroughly enjoyed learning. His unquenchable thirst
for knowledge was evident to the very end of his life. On the day
he died, atop his nightstand lay a hand-written note with a dozen
words and their definitions. He read voraciously on a wide range
of subjects. He was interested in business, science, politics, art,
music, and technology to name a few.

Dad loved science because it is based on a set of established
facts and basic laws. Science made sense to him because it is
provable knowledge. He touted the book *The Bible as History*
because, among other things, it had a scientific explanation for the
parting of the Red Sea.

To Dad, nature represented a universal big picture of order

and beautiful reoccurring patterns. Dad appreciated anything he could concretely see, smell, touch, hear or taste.

He had an interest in all things mechanical. He was an inventor and problem solver. Often, he would quip, "That is the greatest piece of machinery I have ever seen. What does it do?" Or "No problem. With a little modification, this will work great!"

He was interested in the latest medical innovations. Commenting on his new heart valve, he stated, "The valve is excellent. It has a lifetime guarantee."

He appreciated fine art and music. He had definite opinions about excellence in music. "Rachmaninoff will last through the ages! The Beatles, on the other hand, are a flash in the pan, they will never last!" Often, he was right, sometimes, very wrong.

As a senior, he decided he wanted to improve his memory. One day, light in his eyes, he told me about a great book called *The Memory Book*. He went on to say, "With this new method, I am able to remember a list of fifteen items."

"Wow Dad, I would really like to read it. May I borrow it?"

Feeling trapped, his lips began to quiver. His eyes moved wildly back and forth as he tried to find workable words to explain the situation. I waited.

"Well… uh, no," he sputtered. "I don't have the book anymore."

Eyebrows raised, I waited. A look of bleak desperation crossed his face and then his expression tightened in defensive resolve. "I had a lot on my mind... I left the book on the top of the car and drove off."

I couldn't help it. I laughed.

At the end of a small chuckle, Dad emphatically stated, "Well...uh... it was a really good book!"

"I'm sure it was, Dad, I'm sure it was!"

Even in the hardest of times, Dad saw his glass as half full. He had a saying for every occasion. For example, Dad had a myriad of answers to the question, "How are you feeling?" If he was feeling good, the answer was, "Like a young gazelle." If he was feeling bad, he would say, "Like the bottom of the furnace." If the weather was too hot, it was, "I'm so hot, I am nearly bacon... I never sausage heat." If he was in the middle of a project, he would say, "I am as busy as a Bird dog."

After Dad died, my brother, Brad, wrote about his eternal optimism. "If Dad burned his toast, he would simply scrape off the black and claim it was 'just the way I like it.' If things came a little too easily to him in the first half of his life, the latter part was overly difficult. But he never gave up, never complained, never stopped dreaming fresh dreams. He just scraped off the burnt part and said life was just the way he liked it."

Dad owned a thriving propane company in Montana. We moved to Oregon when I was six years old. From the age of six until I was in my twenties, Dad owned and ran a highly successful fertilizer company. I believe a series of small strokes called TIAs (transient ischemic attacks), a constant search for new challenges and opportunities, and bad business decisions led to Dad's financial downfall. Since Dad believed "security is for cadavers" and "money is the chips you play with in the business game," he wasn't overly concerned.

Dad's mind resided in a swirl of clouds. He was often oblivious to the effect his actions had on others. His fierce dedication to optimism, his loyalty to the facts and figures of science, and his fear of feelings often prevented from connecting or empathizing with others. Although losing his wealth didn't faze him, it did have a huge effect on Mom and their marriage. After twenty-five years of marriage, Mom asked for a divorce. It was pretty clear, Dad still loved Mom. One time, after divorced about five years, Dad talked to me about their relationship. "Your mother and I had the perfect marriage."

"Dad, perfect marriages don't usually end in divorce."

"This one did!"

Throughout his later years, despite the divorce and financial hardship, Dad kept his sense of humor. After the divorce, he invited a woman over for a meal. His date was to bring the hors d'oeuvres.

"Phil," she asked, "do you have any toothpicks for my appetizers?"

"I'm sorry," he said. "I'm fresh out. I lost all the toothpicks in the divorce."

One day, Dad was reminiscing about his years as a very successful businessman. "Life has been just great; I had twenty years of a really good run."

The loss of wealth never seemed to affect Dad's self-esteem. As a senior, he happily lived in low-income housing. One day he stopped by sister Leslie's house to visit us. After a short stay, Dad said he had to get back to his apartment. "Why? What is the hurry?"

"I am invited to a party."

"Really?" I said.

A little embarrassed, he said, "Yes, five women and me." His face brightened. "I guess I'm still quite a hunk." As he jumped in his beater station-wagon, he waved goodbye, "See ya 'round the mill."

When Dad would visit Yokes and me, the conversation was

never dull. On one occasion, the topic of therapy was broached. Of course, Dad had an opinion. "I suppose therapy could benefit some, but I can't see how it would help me."

Dad was implying he was too smart for therapy to work.

As a psychotherapist, I stayed silent, waiting to see what would happen.

My husband replied, "Well, Phil, that's an interesting premise. I think of myself as fairly intelligent."

"Oh yes, you are very intelligent."

"I know for a fact therapy saved my life."

At this point, Dad's lips begin to quiver. He nodded his head in understanding, mumbled something, and changed the subject.

Later, driving with Dad through a snowstorm, he again brought up the subject of therapy.

"About this therapy business."

"Yes, Dad?"

"I really could benefit from therapy, but I will never try it because feelings scare the hell out of me."

"Thank you, Dad, for sharing!"

The doctors predicted Dad's heart valve would last for ten years. They were right. Dad's heart gave out at the age of seventy-four.

On learning he was terminal, Dad wrote a letter to the family:

Dear family,

There is an old adage "if you take care of your body, it will take care of you." So far, we're about even! Am going by the progressive statement of my family "Dad, you're looking great." If this keeps up, when the end comes, I should be stunning! No longer do I have a mind like a steel trap. I realize I can no longer whip a grizzly bear with a stick and this somewhat flabby veneer on my body doesn't necessarily cover a massive superstructure of sinewy muscular development. Still there are hopes and unrealized dreams to contend with. I can still imagine myself stepping in a phone booth and emerging with a big S stenciled on my T-shirt.

So, if they have to feed me through a feeding tube and I can't at least come back with a little quip "good, but I thought the roast beef was a little tough." It will show all concerned that I'm under strain and desire that you pull the plug. Hell, I don't want to live if I can't hit it full bell. I will simply fold my tent and steal away.

Just turn out the lights and let me paddle the rest of the way.

Signed,
P C Bird

His fast-moving big picture stilled in the last year of his life. His busy brain came down from the clouds and landed softly on earth. He began to notice and appreciate small, wondrous things: a child playing, a kindness, a courtesy, a smile, a laugh, a touch. He was finally able to share and receive feelings of love. In the end he experienced peace on this earth, so he could live the true big picture in heaven. I love you, Dad. See ya 'round the mill.

7
What's in a Name?

It was August 1945, and there was much to celebrate on the Sioux Indian reservation. World War II had ended, and a new baby girl was welcomed into the world. The baby's birth was extra special because she was delivered by her own great grandmother, the community's midwife.

The only person who wasn't happy about the birth was Ginny, the baby's mother. She was a twenty-three-year-old, full-blooded Sioux Indian who, after a fling with a Caucasian of Italian descent, ended up pregnant. Ginny did not want to talk about him. His name, listed as the father on the baby's birth certificate, was the only proof of his existence. The baby inherited her grandfather's and mother's last name: Goodteacher.

Ellen Goodteacher flourished on the reservation. She was a well-loved member of her tribe. A group of relatives and community members watched over her. The teachings of the Episcopal church, as well as Indian legends passed down through generations, gave her a good moral and spiritual foundation. Ellen loved to learn! There were great teachers everywhere: schoolteachers, church clergy and doctrine, people in the community, and books! Reading was her passion, and she savored every little morsel of knowledge on almost any subject.

Ellen was three when her mother married. Ginny Goodteacher became Ginny Whipple. In the eight years that followed, Ginny gave Ellen two half-brothers and a half-sister. She loved her siblings but had a volatile relationship with her mother and disliked her abusive, alcoholic stepfather. Ellen was glad she was still a Goodteacher—she definitely didn't want to be a Whipple. She was also glad to be growing up in the protective cocoon of the reservation.

Ellen's protection ended when her parents decided to participate in a new government program. The family was taken off the reservation and relocated to Denver. Ellen, at eleven, was taken from her nurturing community. She hated Denver and fiercely missed her old home.

She took on the mother role in earnest when she was twelve and her baby sister was born. She wanted her siblings to feel the safety and love she received on the reservation. Re-creating a safe feeling for them in Denver was hard, but Ellen had a big heart. She watched over her brothers and sisters, showering them with love. To create a semi-safe world for herself, she buried herself in books.

Junior high, the age of rebellion, found Ellen pregnant at the age of fourteen. Toby Garcia was eighteen. Ginny insisted she go to a facility for unwed mothers and give the baby away. Ellen refused. Lashing out at her mother, she yelled, "My baby will feel loved and wanted. My baby won't feel rejected like you reject me. I'll be a good mother." She then went to the bathroom to throw up. The vomiting could have been a reaction to her mother, but most likely a case of severe morning sickness. The ongoing morning sickness caused her to drop out of school in the ninth grade.

Toby's mother demanded that her son marry Ellen. Her future mother-in-law planned and paid for the entire wedding. Because of Ellen's young age, Ginny had to sign the marriage certificate. Ellen was furious when she found out her mother had signed her name as Ellen Whipple.

For nineteen years, Ellen was married to Toby, a gambler and alcoholic. While married, Ellen Garcia raised four kids: three children of her own and her nephew. In response to the death of Ellen's stepfather, her mother had a breakdown. Ginny began to drink alcoholically and was in and out of mental institutions, which left her baby sister without a mother. So Ellen, caregiver extraordinaire, took in and raised her youngest sibling for three years.

Being a good mother wasn't the only job Ellen took seriously. The destructive cycle of addiction permeated her life. In addition to her husband's alcoholism, drug and alcohol problems gripped the lives of all her siblings. Even some of her own children were showing signs of dependency. Ellen, in her early thirties, would waste no more time. It would be her mission, from here on out, to do everything in her power to save lives by fighting addiction. Because she knew knowledge was power, she studied and received her GED. Her next step was to create a healthy environment for herself and her kids. She divorced her gambler, alcoholic husband and was a free woman before her twentieth wedding anniversary.

For the next thirty years, Ellen faced many challenges. Some she won, and some she lost. Her goal was to never give up and to learn from each conflict. At the age of thirty-five, she garnered her first job as a counselor in the addiction field. Despite having no formal education in addiction treatment, she was hired. She had absolutely no idea why she got the job. Maybe being surrounded by addiction most of her life counted for something. Did her interviewers notice her eagerness to learn or consider the fact she had read many books on the subject? She didn't know. Whatever the reason, she was grateful, because she loved her job. Ellen proved to be a natural counselor and teacher.

At the age of forty-four, she received her BA in human services with an emphasis on drug and alcohol. Nine years later, she received her Master's in Social Work. Armed with treatment experience, knowledge, and degrees, she saved lives by teaching others how to recognize and break the addictive cycle.

She would reward her hard work by taking back her identity. Her mother, stepfather, and ex-husband would never again have power to define her. She was no longer a Whipple or Garcia. At age fifty, without telling a soul, she became Ellen Goodteacher once again. Anyone who knows her will tell you the name Goodteacher recognizes her talents, describes her essence, and fits her to a T.

In her fifties and sixties, she mentored college students in their role as social workers in agency and school settings. Ellen also worked for four years in the social work department of the college in which she received her BA. She could rest easy now. Her life was set, she had achieved her mission, she liked her profession, and loved taking back her name.

Little did she know, her life was about to drastically change. For years, she tried to help her youngest son, John, deal with his addiction to alcohol and meth. Because he wasn't interested in getting clean, she made the healthy decision to detach. Rumor had it, his girlfriend was pregnant. Months had passed with no contact from John until Ellen received a phone call at work. "Mom, my girlfriend is having the baby. Could you come to the hospital?"

A short time later, Amanda was born. Ellen remembers

holding her granddaughter in her arms. "I bonded with her immediately. In an instant, she grabbed my heart and changed my life." Ellen had come full circle. Her new purpose in life was to love, protect, and teach this precious gift from God.

Sadly, Amanda's biological mother was using drugs throughout her pregnancy. Amanda was born with methamphetamines and THC in her system. Her birth mother showed no interest in staying clean. After a failed attempt at becoming a family, Amanda's parents separated, resulting in Amanda and John moving in with Ellen. Soon after they moved in, Ellen strongly suspected her son was using drugs again. John's erratic behavior and abuse of Amanda were unacceptable, and she asked him to leave. It seemed clear to Ellen that neither parent had the ability or desire to raise their little girl.

Ellen received custody, then legal guardianship, of her granddaughter. She retired and is now a hard-working, full-time grandmother. Church, family, friends, support groups, teachers, counselors, books, and other resources have all helped Ellen raise Amanda. Hopefully, the addictive cycle has been broken. The cycle of love is in full force.

Today, Amanda is a smart, healthy, active child who loves to read. She is, however, eleven. Ellen remembers being eleven and has great compassion for its trials and tribulations. At the age of seventy-five, Ellen is more determined than ever to persevere and to gain some knowledge from every conflict. For her part, as a preteen, Amanda has taken seriously her responsibility to teach her grandmother patience. Most of the time, Ellen Goodteacher still loves to learn, if she's not too tired.

8
All in the Family

"Like father, like son" is a familiar phrase used to describe similarities. For the most part, I really like the alike traits of my husband and his father. I would, however, firmly place in the dislike category my feelings toward my husband's and father-in-law's stubborn attitude about physical health. I have two stories that go to the heart of the issue.

The first involves my now eighty-eight-year-old father-in-law. Two and a half years ago, when Don was a spry eighty-five-, almost eighty-six-year-old, I was tasked with accompanying him to a cardiologist at the behest of his general practitioner. Don informed the heart doctor that he felt fine and he believed in the old adage "if it ain't broke, don't fix it." The cardiologist, after listening to his heart, said the whooshing sound of the blood was so loud, he could hear it without a stethoscope. The doctor recommended some tests, because he strongly suspected a heart valve was "broke" (using Don's vernacular) and needed to be "fixed." Sure enough, after many tests, it was determined Don needed a valve replacement.

Another cardiologist recommended an orthoscopic procedure called transcatheter aortic valve replacement (TAVR) to fix the problem. Compared to open-heart surgery, this procedure is less invasive with a far shorter recovery time. The catch was… two heart surgeons and a cardiologist had to agree the procedure was needed. Even though Don didn't have energy to take a shower, he was still walking for short distances under his own steam. In the opinion of two heart surgeons, he didn't qualify for TAVR because his condition wasn't severe enough. My husband, jumping through major hoops, sought a second opinion.

Don needed more tests and more doctor visits. Although he didn't want open-heart surgery, he wasn't helping his case. Don had a severe aversion to appearing weak. His fear of being labeled a hypochondriac was on par with death. His response to the numerous doctors we visited, was consistent. "How are you feeling today, Don?" the doctor would question. Don's answer was always the same: "Fine." Finally, I had a heart-to-heart with Don.

"Don, if you want open-heart surgery, continue to say you are feeling fine. If you would like the TAVR, don't say fine."

The next doctor we visited asked, "How are you feeling today, Don?"

"Fi—" Don started to say. He stopped mid-word. A look of wide-eyed panic crossed his face as he searched for another answer. Finally, lighting on a possible response, he calmed, set his chin and proudly answered, "I'm here."

The result: Don finally figured out his priorities and was able to have a successful TAVR procedure. Today, at the age of eighty-eight, he states he is feeling "fine!" And for the most part, I believe, he is finally telling the truth.

His son, my husband (carrying his father's DNA and attitude), had a similar heart incident years earlier at the age of fifty-seven. The time was the middle of March 2010, right in the heart of busy season for my CPA husband. We were walking through our hilly neighborhood when he stopped suddenly, his face scrunched up in pain.

"What's wrong?" I asked.

"You don't want to know," he answered.

I gave my typical female answer. "Yes, I really do want to know."

An angry, annoyed look crossed his face. I waited. He gave me an exasperated sigh. "It's nothing…probably just busy-season stress." I waited. "I will call the doctor if it gets worse."

Not knowing what "it" was exactly, but knowing enough not to press the issue, I waited. I waited until the early morning hours when Yokes bolted out of bed and crumpled to the floor. Tired of waiting, I suggested calling 911.

Through gritted teeth, my husband gave me the "I-will-kill-you if-you-dare" look. "It will be all right. We can call the clinic in the morning."

Still not knowing what "it" was, but suspecting it was bad, I decided I would call the clinic the minute it opened. I called at 8:30 AM on the dot and handed my exhausted husband the phone (pain is exhausting). He made an appointment with our regular doctor for 3:30 PM. He then began to answer questions about symptoms. He was finally explaining "it" as "intense pain, pain shooting down my arm, pain that takes my breath away." Hanging up the phone, he went downstairs to his office to do tax returns.

Five minutes later, the clinic called and asked me to put him on the phone. He put clinic personnel on speakerphone in order to keep doing tax returns. I heard, "Dr. Matthews wants you to call 911. He doesn't want you to wait until 3:30. He wants you to call 911 now."

"This is not a good time. I am a CPA in busy season."

The answer was succinct. "We will not be responsible for your death. Call 911."

Exasperated sigh… "Oh, all right, if you insist, I'll call."

The ambulance came. Yokes took a break from tax returns to receive an EKG. The EKG was abnormal, causing the EMTs to recommend going in the ambulance to a nearby hospital.

Yokes' computer was making loud "get-back-to-work" noises. He distractedly responded, "that won't be necessary, Bird will drive me." (Bird is my last name. My husband calls me Bird as a term of endearment, but at this moment it was…something else.)

I decided, this would be the opportune time to stop waiting and speak up. "Right, Yokes." (His last name is Yocum… this is sometimes a term of endearment and sometimes not.) "You would like me, a high-risk driver, to drive you to the hospital when you are at high risk for having a heart attack? Really?"

Yokes stopped listening to his computer, turned toward the medics and sheepishly said, "I've changed my mind. I will go in the ambulance." Then he looked at me again. "Bird, bring my computer. Meet me at the hospital."

"It" turned out to be the left descending artery that was 94% blocked. After receiving a stent, he was lying in his hospital bed, computer on his lap, doing a tax return.

"Wow, what a close call."

He looked up from his computer and said with a smile, "What are you talking about? I had a good six percent to go before a heart attack."

Much like his father, my husband's response to a physical crisis is exasperating, irritating, and mysterious. Bottom line—I love him and want him to continue his life cycle. Next time, I'm thinking of calling 911. "Over my dead body," Yokes might say. I will ignore him, because no matter what he says, I know in his heart he has his priorities straight. In the end, I know, given a choice, both father and son will continue to choose life!

9
Growing Up Together

The beginning of their marriage was golden. She was thirty-eight, he was forty. Both had great careers, Marilyn as a flight attendant, Jim as a sportscaster. Love and laughter filled their days. They traveled together extensively. Even their time away from each other was nearly perfect. Marilyn had time to herself when he worked evenings; Jim had time when she traveled. In the first several years of marriage, the relationship blossomed. The bond formed was firmly rooted in their shared spirituality. They both believed life to be a positive process for learning lessons and viewed every lesson as an opportunity to learn and grow. In their early marriage, they happily and lovingly danced down easy street, laughing all the way.

Easy street turned into a bumpy road when Jim caught a life-altering virus that knocked the breath right out of the once strong, active jock. Jim had a mind-over-matter response to his illness. His mind didn't allow him to be sick. He willed himself to get up every morning and plaster on a normal, healthy face to the world. His body and Marilyn disagreed with his mind's assessment; the man's immune system had been compromised.

In the years that followed, the bumpy road became a bit

rockier. Continental Airlines closed their Denver base, requiring Marilyn to seek a career change. She pursued a career in skin care. Their well-choreographed routine was forever changed. Not to be deterred, this couple continued their lifestyle of fun-filled travel and laughter. There were, however, brief periods of trouble. Jim's denial almost always accompanied his bouts of severe infections and illnesses. With Jim's denial came Marilyn's bouts of helplessness and depression.

This rocky road slowly narrowed into a steep, winding path strewn with large obstacles. After more than two decades of loving his career as a TV sportscaster, Jim began to dread going to work. His profession was losing its heart and becoming corporate. He resigned. Jim found other employment, but the loss of his career was heartbreaking. In one fell swoop, he had lost his identity, his standing as a public figure, his financial security, and a profession he loved.

The loss of his health was perhaps the most debilitating. At one point, following his fourth sinus surgery, an infection almost killed him. While on a home IV for three months, Jim's mind began to acknowledge what his body and Marilyn had known for a long time; he was really sick. He was thankful he was alive and grateful for the lesson. He learned he had to acknowledge his illness in order to heal. He also became more keenly aware of

Marilyn's dedication and sacrifice in dealing with his health. He was open to her suggestions. Marilyn, no longer invisible, was able to give herself credit for the hard work.

For the first time, Marilyn talked to a professional about her experience living with Jim and his illness. She was immediately validated by the psychiatrist. He said fifteen years of hearing her husband's nonstop cough was incredibly difficult and exhausting. She had done an admirable job and had paid her dues. Another lesson learned. Jim and Marilyn began to join forces and confront together any obstacle standing in the way of a healthy life.

The team seemed to be on firm ground until Jim, not paying attention to his personal responsibilities, lost his footing and began a downhill slide. He knocked Marilyn over in the process. Jim had done the unthinkable and let his medical insurance lapse. Marilyn was livid. She packed a bag to stay overnight with a friend. While unpacking, she noticed she only brought one slipper. She was swearing up a storm about the slipper when Jim called. He apologized profusely, said he loved her, and had a plan to solve the problem. He told her they could get through anything together. She returned home to find Jim and her matching slipper. After all, they are a great pair!

The lessons just kept on coming. Jim's medical bills plus years of not adjusting their lifestyle and spending habits ultimately led to bankruptcy. As a couple they chose to make the uphill climb to financial solvency.

At present, they have reached a relationship pinnacle, and the view is spiritually breathtaking! Jim is healing physically. Together, they are healing emotionally and financially. They are both so thankful for the lessons. When I asked Marilyn to summarize their relationship, she laughed her joyous laugh. She then simply said, "We came together to help each other grow up! We never needed anything more." Today, she is sixty-seven, he is sixty-nine, and their marriage is now truly golden.

10
Happy Camper

Laura's husband Steve had the biggest heart. He loved helping people. If a philanthropic organization needed help, he was there, bringing his energy and experience to any project. At least ten nonprofit organizations benefited from his expertise in website development. He was a multi-faceted man: a realtor, a webpage designer, a fun RV camper and adventurer, and a nature lover. Most importantly, he was a dedicated husband, father, and friend.

Laura and Steve were married right after college. Their adult lives were fulfilling—busy with their two sons, careers, friends, and community. They entered their senior years full of hope and happiness. They settled in a small mountain community. Their big, beautiful home sat in the middle of a forested piece of land— their patch of serenity. The wonders of nature surrounded them.

The highlight of their summers was to jump in their RV and travel around the country with their friends. They loved everything involved in these adventures: planning the trip, getting ready, driving, and setting up camp. In the evenings, Laura looked forward to cooking, Steve liked the outdoor guy chores, and they both loved sitting around the campfire with friends. By day, they enjoyed hiking and exploring new places. Physically, it seemed,

Laura and Steve were doing well. She was pretty much pain-free, having had a successful back surgery years earlier. Laura wasn't too concerned about Steve's health either; he was an active guy and an avid hiker to boot. She had on occasion, encouraged him to take better care of himself. He could stand to lose some weight, and he would, when he decided the time was right.

In the fall, winter, and spring Laura taught elementary-school children. In addition to working as a Realtor, Steve was busy with all sorts of projects. Because a big mortgage accompanied the big home, Laura was a little concerned about finances. Steve reassured her, saying, "You don't need to worry. I have many irons in the fire." After almost forty-eight years of marriage, Laura had every faith that things would work out, they always had in the past. Steve had never failed her!

The year was 2014, the month, October. Laura rose early to get ready for school. She smiled as she read Steve's note from the night before "It's snowing big flakes!" Steve's sweet communication to his wife was his last on earth. He died of a massive heart attack that morning. He was gone, and Laura's life was turned upside down.

The outpouring of love from family and friends was immediate. On the day of the funeral, Laura's school principal closed down the school for a half day for all those who wished to attend the memorial. The pastor of Laura and Steve's church helped put together a wonderful service.

When family and friends, who had gathered together to honor Steve, gradually went back to their lives, Laura was left empty in a big house filled to the brim with reminders of her husband. A black cloud of sorrow cast a heavy shadow over her. Numb and in shock, she used the little energy she had putting one foot in front of the other, as she trudged through her days.

She felt like she was being buried under an avalanche of urgent responsibilities, unfinished business, and important tasks. Her friends and family initially tried to offer support by suggesting ways to handle grief. Groups, therapy, books, and talking about feelings were mentioned. Laura knew they were just trying to be helpful. She also knew listening to her heart and trusting her judgment, would put her on the right path to healing. She was an independent and private person; she would grieve on her terms, in her time, and in her way. She believed it was up to the individual to decide what was best. She also believed she would not only survive the death of her husband, but eventually find happiness in her new life. Fortunately, her friends and family gave her the space to grieve, and the support she needed in her everyday life.

First things first—she had to be practical. She had to figure out ways to climb out of her financial hole. Two weeks after the funeral, she went back to her teaching job. Her work brought in some money, kept her busy, and provided a temporary distraction from her grief and fiscal concerns. The thought of selling the house was overwhelming, but it had to be done. Day after day she would arrive home after work exhausted. Upon entering the house, she would search for Steve. Reality would hit her, and it would feel, for a moment, like she was being crushed under mountains of feelings and insurmountable problems. "You can do anything you set your mind to," she would sternly say to herself. Then she would go to work sifting and sorting through the mountain of stuff her husband left behind. She loved her husband with all her heart, but she wished he hadn't been such a packrat. Her son, Sean, who lived close by, was a godsend. He spent countless hours helping her do whatever needed to be done to get the house ready to sell. Many friends helped as well. She was so grateful for their love and support. They made the process bearable.

Sometimes, in the evenings, sitting alone, her feelings would boil to the surface, and she would have to let them out. She would scream, "Why did you leave me? How could you leave our boys? I'm really mad at you! You left me with a giant mess to clean up. Did you have to be such a packrat? Why didn't you take better care of yourself? How am I supposed to handle all these financial problems? Come back!"

She would cry, "I miss you so much. I love you so much. Your sons miss their dad. We have to sell the house we loved. Some days, I feel so alone and overwhelmed. I wish you were here. I would give anything to go camping with you again."

Did her crying and screaming jags help her? She didn't know. Some nights she felt the tension drain from her body. At these times, she felt at peace and was able to sleep. Some nights, she just felt drained, but the tension remained. When this happened, she was in for a long, sleepless night of worrying. She had unshakable faith her storm would pass, and life would right itself again. Even with this firmly held belief, in the early months after Steve's death, it seemed like every day was Groundhog Day.

Three months after Steve's death, she was invited to visit her son Tim and his family in Australia for Christmas. What a welcome reprieve! She came back home with new energy. She realized her hard work was paying off. The house could soon be put on the market.

Looking out the window one winter's evening, she noticed it was snowing big flakes. The next morning, a bright ball of sun sat in a deep blue Colorado sky beckoning Laura to come outside. A blanket of pristine white snow covered the ground. Hearing the friendly crunch of her boots on the snow, breathing the fresh air, and smelling the evergreens, Laura knew she was on the right path.

Bit by bit, Laura's life improved. As the snow melted and the rivers came full, she sold their large RV. The trees were flowering when she sold the house and lived with friends until she found a smaller place in her beloved mountain community. She hiked among the wildflowers and bought a condo. As the aspens turned to gold, she bought a dog and a small RV.

Six years after Steve's death, she is retired from school teaching, tutors dyslexic children in reading, and has a part-time job as a salesclerk at a fun store. Although she misses Steve every day, she has met someone. He is lots of fun, and a good companion.

In the summers, she jumps in her RV and travels the country with her friends. Amazingly, Laura does all the jobs Steve did as well as the ones she preferred, all the while enjoying nature and hiking. She laughs her big laugh, saying, "If you are determined, you will find a way to do anything you choose to do." Only occasionally will she ask for help backing up the trailer.

The year was 2020. When I asked her how she felt today, she replied immediately. "I am happy." Laura is, indeed, a happy camper.

11
Sleep, Seniors, Sleep

~

Attitude Adjustment

In late August of 2014, I noticed a change in my sixty-two-year-old husband. The active, upbeat husband of old appeared sluggish, listless and fatalistic. "I feel like I'm slogging in mud. I don't know how much longer I will be around. I feel like I'm dying."

Our amazing GP suspected sleep apnea. Mud-slogging continued for both Yokes and the process due to constant insurance and appointment delays. Finally, National Jewish Hospital confirmed the diagnosis, stating Yokes stopped breathing 99 times an hour while sleeping. Since breathing shouldn't be overrated and is essential to living, no wonder my husband thought he was dying. The hospital ordered the desperately needed breathing machine called the APAP. January of 2015, we were told the machine was supposed to arrive any day. I wasn't holding my breath.

Slow-forward to one dark, cold evening in the middle of January. It was late. ("Late," for a couple in their sixties, is a relative term.) I had just arrived home after a meeting and glanced at the clock in the kitchen. 10:15. Yep. Late.

Being the good wife that I am, I tiptoed through the house knowing my husband would probably be in bed. I was right, the lights were off in the bedroom. I stopped... I could hear a strange sound emanating from inside. I have a significant hearing loss, yet the sound was loud and unsettling. Slowly, I opened the door and hesitantly approached the bed. Our yellow nightlight garishly colored an otherworldly figure lying in our bed. I jumped back. Instead of seeing my sweet husband's face, a ghostly, disembodied, Darth-Vader-like masked head (albeit white) lay atop the covers. The loud, throaty breathing coming from the apparition almost caused me to panic, thinking this must be an alien invasion! But, coming to my senses, I realized the APAP machine we were waiting for must have been delivered today. With this logical explanation becoming clear in my mind, my heart rate returned to earth.

I readied myself for bed, pondering the best way to cope with my radically different-looking sleeping partner and environment. My thought process was suddenly drenched in a tidal-wave hot flash/night sweat combination that drowned out all thoughts of optimism. Lying flat on my back, looking up at the ceiling, I asked myself, "Where is the silver lining in this?" Just then a miracle happened. My sweet, masked man turned over on his side, hitting me with a blast of cold air. This instantly dissolved my night sweats and warmed me to my new environment and my husband's new image. "Yes, this will work," I thought as I drifted off to sleep.

In the middle of the night, I awakened with a start and another dilemma. It is true, I wanted my husband to breathe. The problem—my husband is extremely bright without this breathing appliance. My thought was, "With the APAP, how will I ever be able to win another game? My self-esteem might take a huge hit… Maybe I need to go into therapy for this issue. No, too drastic… Maybe I'll think about it tomorrow." I did—and the day after and for months… Until my husband had a knee replacement.

In the early days of his recovery, we were playing cards. In his drugged state, he fell asleep while dealing, and I won that game! The moral of these stories: If you choose to see it, there is always a senior silver lining. Sometimes instantaneous; sometimes you just have to be patient.

Rituals

The following is based on a true story of one particular couple. Warning: The action sequences may vary depending on the ages, situation and health of the couple.

Remember the old nighttime ritual when you were young? It went something like this: whine, remove clothes and shoes, jump into jammies, brush teeth, wash face, pee, hop into bed, sleep eight hours.

When whittling down this routine into action words, what remains is a simple sequence of events. A kid typically takes eight nighttime actions: whine, remove, jump, brush, wash, pee, hop, sleep.

For the bedtime ritual of a senior couple, I have broken down the bedtime routine into just three easy steps; ready, get set, sleep.

Ready:

The ready step starts in the TV room and ends up in the master bath and closet.

The husband's ready step is as follows: falls asleep watching TV, wife wakes him, he whines, climbs stairs to bedroom, removes shoes and clothes, puts on jammies, Waterpiks teeth, brushes teeth, pees.

The wife's ready step is as follows: watches TV while husband sleeps, wakes up husband, climbs stairs to bedroom, swallows pills, injects self with osteoporosis drug, cleanses and hydrates face, brushes teeth for two minutes, gargles, spits, takes off orthotics-filled shoes, removes clothes, puts on lounge bralette and jammies, fills up water glass, puts in mouth splint, pees.

Get set:

The get-set step takes place in the master bedroom.

The husband's get set routine: throws throw pillows, turns down covers on his side of the bed, fills up APAP with distilled water, turns on oxygen concentrator, sits on bed and slathers feet and hands with lotion, lies down, puts on mask, turns off light, reads in the dark on his iPhone in defiance of the literature. (The literature states electronic devices emit blue light, which delays the production of melatonin and can lead to insomnia and poor sleep.) Nevertheless, he falls asleep with reading glasses on and iPhone in hand.

The wife's get-set routine: brings water glass to nightstand, gently places throw pillows on floor, turns down covers on her side of the bed, closes shades, turns on fan, takes off glasses, takes out hearing aids, puts in battery charger, lotions hands, puts on lip gloss, lies down, turns off light, sometimes reads iPad in defiance of literature.

Sleep:

The husband's sleep regimen is: falls asleep with glasses on and iPhone in hand, drops iPhone, sleeps for about five hours.

The wife's sleep regimen is: gets hot, kicks off covers, gets cold, pulls up covers, gets hot, kicks off covers, gets cold, pulls up covers, gets thirsty, drinks water, gets up, pees, comes back to bed, and the cold/hot routine resumes. The restless sleep extends for seven to eight hours.

Sleep Sequences

Watches, sleeps, wakes
Whines, climbs
Throws

Piks, brushes, gargles
Swallows, spits
Close

Cleanses, lotions, needles
Sits, slathers
Lies

Puts in, takes out, fills up
Takes off, puts on
Pees

Turns off, turns on, turns down
Pulls up, kicks off
Reads

Pees, drinks, pees
Pulls up, kicks off
Sleeps

This senior couple's sleep sequence is exhausting. Is it worth it? Yes!

This is where the story ends. I don't want to even think about what is involved in the morning wake-up ritual.

12

The Voice of Spirit

As a small child, Angela remembers the competing sounds of her parents' voices. The warm and gentle voice of her mother wrapped her in a blanket of peace and love. Her mother would hum and sing throughout the day. In Angela's mind, her mother's music painted a picture of a bright, sweet-smelling field of wildflowers—a world filled with joy and hope.

Frequently her mother's voice was drowned out by the loud, mean and hateful voice of her father. His demeaning tirades were always scary. Even more terrifying was the possibility these outbursts would lead to physical abuse. Most of the time they didn't, but sometimes they did. Usually, after one of her father's episodes, Angela's world became steeped in silence and hopelessness. Thankfully, soon after an incident always came the sound of her mother's joyful singing. The cycle continued: a clash of two competing voices.

Angela consciously realized the power of her spirit when she was six years old. The four of them were a half-mile from their farmhouse. Her mother and father were stripping cotton. Her father was screaming at her mother for not keeping up. Her three-month-old baby brother was sobbing uncontrollably. Angela was terrified. What would happen to her mom?

"Angela, take your brother home." Angela nodded and mumbled a soft, "OK." She was scared, but she had to be strong. She had to help her mom. She would do her part and take her baby brother home. She held the shrieking baby in her arms and started her long trek home. Out of her father's range, she began to sing. Her brother immediately calmed, opened his eyes wide, smiled his sweet smile, and fell asleep. She knew in that instant she possessed her very own powerful spirit that couldn't be taken from her no matter what happened. If she could calm a frightened baby, and, in doing so, calm herself, she could do anything. She was very much like her mom; her inner voice spoke words of love, not fear.

I met Angela when she was forty-two. We were neophyte therapists working at a community center. I was drawn to her immediately. Her full-throated laugh was contagious. Her non-judgmental attitude was refreshing, but it was her serenity, the depth of love emanating from her soul, that calmed me and gave me courage to deal with my problems. We became fast friends.

Thirty years later, Angela journeyed with her husband to the Mount Princeton Hot Springs. She suffers from arthritis, and the hot pools help with the pain. For Angela, the hotter the better; she picked the 105° pool. Her husband, not being able to handle that kind of heat, left for another pool. When he returned, he found his unresponsive wife floating face down in the water. The paramedics were on the scene quickly. When she regained consciousness, she found herself lying on the lounge chair surrounded by paramedics and a concerned husband. All dignity lost, she felt she might just die of embarrassment. The feeling was fleeting as more pressing issues arose. She was really sick, with every breath causing excruciating pain.

She contemplated slipping into the blackness; after all, death by hot pool isn't the worst way to go. "No, I'm not ready to die. I love life. I am not done living. Nothing will take my life without a fight. Death will be on my terms." At the age of six Angela learned for certain her spirit was stronger than any kind of trauma or pain. Now she took one breath, then another and another until she filled her lungs with life-sustaining air. She was grateful for the experience. It was a gift to her.

She learned death was real, and she didn't ever want to take life for granted. From that day forward, she would always consume great quantities of water when in a hot pool. Evidently, dehydration was the precursor to her near-death experience.

A year and a half later, she was diagnosed with stage III lung cancer. Her doctor gave her a 50-50 chance of surviving six months to two years. She told the doctors she had never cared much for statistics. Still strong in spirit, she decided to skip worrying about a doctor's opinion and put her energy into living. After months of chemotherapy and radiation to shrink the tumor, she opted for surgery. Post-surgery, she experienced one of the lowest times of her life. She was skin and bones, in immense pain, lying flat on her back, too weak to move. She remembers thinking, "I'm strong enough to deal with death; not dealing with it is not an option. Nobody is in this body but me. I am responsible for how I live and how I die. I will fully face death, so that I may be free to live."

After facing death, her energy and spirit miraculously returned. That was seven years ago, and she is still humming, laughing and loving life.

This is a story of the spirit of a courageous and remarkable woman. She is a gift to me and all who know her!

13

Double Bubble

The four of us met in college. We were definitely a part of a double bubble. All of us grew up in a bubble of safety and security. We ventured out, we thought, into the real world when we went to college. Our parents knew we were entering just another phase of protective bubble wrap. Free from hardship or worry, the university experience was filled with fun adventures, parties, spring breaks in Mexico, and sometimes going to class. We roomed together at different times during and shortly after college, then we each went our separate ways. Although we visited each other on occasion through the years, we were mostly birthday- and Christmas-card friends.

For the next twenty-seven years, life happened to all of us. Each journeyed through careers, child rearing, difficult relationships, moving, loss and family drama. Some of us dealt with marriage, divorce, illnesses, accidents and the effects of addiction.

In the fall of 1999, the first annual get-together happened for Cindy, Cynthia, and me. We were just about to complete our middle-age phase and tumble headlong into seniority. For the next twenty years, we met once a year, to provide a soft landing, a real-world reprieve and an extension of the protective college bubble experienced years before. Some years, getting together was quite a challenge, but we made it happen because it was important. We took turns planning our yearly adventure. In the process, we learned persistence, adaptability, creative scheduling and finances.

Phebe, our fourth college friend, was able to join us in our fourteenth year. We were all in our sixties when she came on board. Sober, clean, and a cancer survivor, she was well-versed in self-care. She added another dimension to our group. She gave us a sense of spirituality and wisdom that comes with years of sobriety and modeled the emotional and physical health she used to beat cancer.

When the four of us would get together, it was caregivers central, featuring a PT, an OT, a grief counselor, and a psychotherapist. In our late forties and early fifties, we would generously share our professional tools.

By the time Phebe came on the scene, the three of us had reached a level of maturity. Caregivers have the notorious reputation of being terrible at self-care, and we were not an exception to this rule. To our credit, we each decided on our own that our get-togethers wouldn't be working vacations.

Cynthia announced that, for her own rest and relaxation, she would no longer be giving massages or hands-on physical therapy. She, however, was totally up for using her PT expertise on her own terms. When she was in the PT mood, Cynthia was quite creative. One time, she used a carton of ice cream to ice down my inflamed shoulder. When Cindy had her knee replacements, Cynthia was available to help with walking and strengthening techniques. She would also supervise the buying of tennis shoes. Both Cynthia and Phebe were known for their experiential group meditation.

Cindy decided focusing on loss and grief didn't fit with her need for a light-hearted, fun, no-stress vacation but if any of us were truly in need, she was there. When Cynthia's husband was dying of cancer, the three of us met to support her in Arizona. Cindy knew just what to say and how to say it. As a thank you, Cynthia bought everyone a ceramic pumpkin complete with a battery-powered light. To this day, when any of our group needs a little extra support, we light our pumpkins.

I needed and wanted an issueless, drama-free vacation every year. I was looking forward to exciting adventures, noticing nature, playing, laughing, and desserts. I was, however, available in crisis situations. One of my more helpful parenting suggestions was to let your child figure things out by limiting your communication to "Wow," "Bummer," "How did you feel about that?" and "I trust you will make the right decision."

What held our friendship together? Love, laughter, food, nature, activities, adventures, and sharing connected us through the years. When friends join together, many emotions bubble up. Every year we each took time to acclimate after arriving from different geographical, physical, and emotional states. Every year, our differences would dissolve and become one big melting pot of love, compassion, and caring support.

Laughter lightened our lives. Both Cindy and Phebe have big, contagious laughs, which made it impossible for Cynthia and me not to be caught up in the merriment. A few laughing examples should tell our tale. We laughed about driving—Cynthia was our designated driver on many of the getaways. Why? Because she was good at it. That meant Cindy and I were the designated navigators. We were not good at it. On an unfamiliar road in New Mexico, we ended up driving forty-five minutes the wrong way, and nobody noticed. We were all laughing hysterically when, that same day, we turned around and provided more faulty navigation, resulting in eleven U-turns.

We laughed about packing: Cindy and Cynthia packing in 110° Arizona heat forgetting to bring a stitch of clothing appropriate for Colorado cold and snow, and me bringing bulky snow boots from Colorado to Arizona at Cynthia's urging. I believe her exact statement was "It might snow in Flagstaff, so bring your boots." I heard snow boots; evidently she meant hiking boots.

We had many examples of funny forgetfulness. Phebe

provided one of the funniest stories. Phebe and I were the last passengers in the baggage claim area. She was concerned her luggage was lost. We discussed how to handle her missing bag while watching a lonely purple suitcase go past on a conveyor belt for the fourth or fifth time. Finally, we decided to check the tag on the bag. It turned out to be Phebe's newly purchased luggage.

We laughed at our eating experiences: at a restaurant, when talking while eating, I was a little bit too expressive and flipped a bite of mushroom ravioli into a candle centerpiece.

Another time, Cindy and I, after a lengthy discussion, decided to split the "volcano," a featured dessert at "World Famous" restaurant in San Diego. The volcano, a chocolate delicacy, was quite expensive and would take twenty minutes to cook. Cindy and I, hankering for chocolate, even decided to come back and pick up our fabulous dessert. Cynthia at that time was into seafood cocktail and wanted no part of our plan. Carrying the big, but light, box holding our precious cargo, we rushed back to our hotel room. The anticipation was palpable as we slowly opened the box. Cindy and I both erupted with laughter. The volcano was so tiny, Cindy and I ate two bites each to finish the entire dessert. Cindy declared the volcano yummy, yummy—one yummy for each bite.

We were taste buddies. In the bubble, we enjoyed many meals and daily discussions about food. We had one who enjoyed meat and vegetables, we had two who liked fish and vegetables, and we had one vegan who could rarely be convinced to stray. One year, we all decided to try vegan, and for the most part we liked it. Three of us were cooks and one a staunch non-cook. Cooking on vacation was optional. The option, in later years, was very rarely used.

S'mores played a significant role in our travels. We were hanging out in my family's Estes Park cabin. Cynthia was contentedly reading a book. Cindy and I, suffering from cabin fever, decided to rummage through the cupboards. To our delight, we found some Hershey bars. Seconds later we came upon some hard marshmallows. The excitement rose to a crescendo when we spied some stale graham crackers. "S'more's!" we squealed. We were screaming so loudly, Cynthia put down her book and came to see what caused the commotion. Cynthia just shook her head as we roasted the marshmallows in the fireplace. From then on, I was in search of the most delectable s'more desserts. I found the best dessert in Sedona. We made a special trip for the s'more specialty a couple years later, only to find they had discontinued my most favorite dessert in the world. When Cindy lost interest, Phebe stepped up. She was sympathetic to my loss. She not only hunted down a s'more dessert in Hilton Head, but also sent me a recipe. I don't do recipes, but I certainly appreciated the effort.

We were nature lovers. In our fifties and early sixties, we

hiked. We hiked in Arizona along meandering streams, among red cliffs and moss rock, through fat, white-trunked aspens thick with golden leaves. In Rocky Mountain National Park, we power-walked around Bear Lake and down a path along a river, through shimmering aspens to a rushing waterfall. The narrow path on the cliffs above the Oregon coast was spectacular! We did some trekking through magnificent rock formations in Kasha-Katuwe Tent Rocks National monument in Santa Fe New Mexico.

Gradually, as we got older, and our bodies started falling apart, we contented ourselves with strolling on the beaches, ambling along a Riverwalk, cruising in a boat on a bay, watching a sunset over a lake, noticing the vibrantly colored fall leaves, and eating meals outside with a view. We even had a fondness for a place we stayed in on a street appropriately named Puddle View. From a window we were able to gaze upon a tiny puddle/pond.

Through our travels we were privy to the sounds and sights of wildlife. We witnessed nature's miracles, from the bugling and sparring of bull elk to the sight and sound of a whale expelling air through its blowhole, to the chattering of many species of birds. We glimpsed bear, moose, deer, alligator, manatee, dolphin, seal, and turtle.

Our activities and adventures varied. In cities, we took in museums, monuments, art galleries, and plays. We laughed hysterically at "Menopause the Musical" and "It's too Loud," featuring music from the seventies and eighties. As seniors, we could relate. Small towns were good for full-body and foot massages, facials, spas, and gentle yoga groups. The group got a good laugh out of a gentle yoga session. Because of a significant hearing loss, I couldn't hear anything the leader was saying. I fell asleep and started snoring. Sometimes the vacation was purely rest and relaxation with not a lot of activity. Oftentimes, when the weather was bad, we would stay in our jammies all day. Card games and Mexican train gave us many hours of fun.

There were a few constants in our vacations. Shopping and eating were pretty fabulous everywhere we went. We varied in our shopping stamina, but to our credit we all tried to be considerate and patient. Sharing was another constant. When our real-world experiences, frustrations, and feelings would bubble up, the love and trust of our group would provide a soft, safe landing for our fears. I wrote all this down. I kept a journal documenting in detail every one of our vacations—the highlights and low lights, our daily activities, and what was happening in our lives. Cindy, Phebe, and I would like to see the journal preserved. Cynthia, being more private, would like to see it burned.

Because of COVID, last year was the first year in twenty-one years we couldn't meet in person. We met several times on Zoom. Connecting remotely doesn't feel remotely like connecting but it's better than nothing! Cynthia and Phebe are both sandwiched between two generations. Taking care of elderly parents while dealing with young adult kids has been challenging. Cynthia's best friend and stress reliever is her dog, Archie. Phebe handles her stress with remote 12-step meetings and taking daily walks with a neighbor.

Cindy has reconnected after fifty-plus years with her first high-school sweetheart. He has been a nice distraction from family drama. Her twin daughters have both had a successful year—one had her first baby, and the other launched her first book.

I have been hanging out with my husband, exercising, skiing, eating desserts, and writing a book for and about seniors.

We are all eternally grateful for the every-year experience in the bubble of love and friendship. I love you Cindy, Cynthia, and Phebe, my double bubble friends.

14
The COVID Corner

The pandemic hit the US in March of 2020. It wreaked havoc on our lives for about a year. The high death rate for those over sixty-five was the greatest concern, but every senior was affected in some way. The COVID corner doesn't represent a cozy chat with a few seniors. This COVID-corner author surveyed many seniors with differing opinions from various parts of the country.

Universal feelings about COVID:

Sadness about all the deaths that occurred during COVID

Empathy for all those who struggled during COVID

Yearning for the freedom to lead a normal life again

Missing loved ones and friends

Extrovert's response to COVID:

Missing human interaction

Established weekly tailgate get-togethers staying six feet apart

Weekly gatherings outside or in garages with neighbors staying six feet apart

Needing to go to the store during senior time to see people

Using senior-time hours to enjoy time away from one's shelter-in-place people

Driving to grocery store parking lot and watching people

Hugging out of habit and feeling guilty about it

Weekly Zoom calls with friends; one senior's group is called "Gab and Guzzle"

Missing travel

Introvert's response to COVID:

Ecstatic to shelter in place

Excuse to stay home

Excited for an excuse not to go to parties, gatherings, celebrations

Don't have to hug anyone

Don't have to travel

Don't have to mingle with people

Don't have to converse with strangers

Not required to make small talk

Don't have to shop

Likes home deliveries

Good aspects of COVID:

Having time to slow down and put things in perspective

Time to reflect on blessings

Grateful for freedoms previously taken for granted

Recovering from having COVID and getting a new lease on life

Development of a vaccine for those who wish to be vaccinated

Able to wear comfy clothes and eat comfort food

Loves the yoga pants and T-shirt uniform

Wearing a mask hides wrinkles and doesn't require make-up

Don't have to buy any new clothes

Learning to entertain oneself

Neighborhoods howling every evening in honor of the first responders

Bad aspects of COVID:

Masks—unable to hear, unable to breathe, unable to see facial expressions, hurts ears

Eating too much leading to weight gain

Had to cook

Unable to go to the gym

Unable to attend church, go to the theater, eat out, attend sporting events

Unable to gather with family and friends

Unable to travel

No funerals, weddings, church gatherings

Runs on toilet paper and other essential items

Hands are raw from too much handwashing and sanitizing

Isolation, loneliness, depression

Too much togetherness from the shelter-in-place situation

Mixed and conflicting messages to seniors about COVID

Bad reaction to the first or second vaccine shot

Unable to get medical screenings, elective surgeries, or dental work

Unable to get a haircut or color

No manicures or pedicures

No massages

What did you do during COVID?

Made multiple masks; one senior made two hundred masks

Not retired yet; worked remotely

Worked on crafts

Cooked

Gardened

Exercised, hiked, walked

Walked the dog(s)

Binge-watched TV series

Learned to use Zoom

Connected with family and friends remotely

De-cluttered

Visited a second home

Saw and hugged family from two different households despite rules

Explored the country in own travel trailer

Read books

Relaxed, reflected, adapted

Stayed grounded

Played computer games

Connected to funny YouTube videos

Wrote a book

15

A Blessed Life

Lynda was in heaven! The year was 1972. She had married her good friend and soulmate, Jerry. They were a young California couple living the dream, spending many happy hours together raising their precious family. Jerry had a fulfilling, well-paying job outside the home. Lynda loved being a stay-at-home mom nurturing their two beautiful daughters, seven-year-old Sandy and three-year-old Tina. She had periodic bouts of depression, but that was normal. She was a fighter, and her love for her girls far outweighed any punch her "down days" could throw at her.

She'd hit a rough spot two years prior. Her mother had died on August 21 of liver cancer at the age of forty-three. Five-year-old Sandy was very sad, but glad her Nan was now happy in heaven. Lynda was also grateful her mother was no longer suffering, but the loss left a huge hole in Lynda's life. For months, she was filled with intense sadness and severe depression. She sought out an Episcopal priest who helped her heal. That part of her life was in the past. At present, life was beautiful, she felt blessed.

In an instant everything changed. There was something definitely wrong with Sandy's right eye. It began to pop out. Immediate surgery was scheduled. The operation revealed a malignant tumor encapsulated in her eye socket. To make matters so much worse, during surgery, a droplet of cancer escaped its capsule, and entered Sandy's body. The cancer spread like wildfire. The doctor gave Lynda the dire diagnosis on August 21, exactly two years after her mother's death.

Within days of the surgery, the cancer had spread to her blood. She had tumors in her lungs and a softball-sized tumor in her liver. The doctors quickly placed her on heavy-duty chemo and radiation therapy. Life for the family completely changed. The happy days of fun art projects and picnics were gone. Suddenly Tina's mom and sister weren't available. Lynda's time was consumed with trips to the hospital and focusing twenty-four-seven on Sandy. Prior to Sandy's diagnosis, Tina was a secure, well-adjusted joyful child. After the diagnosis, she became clingy, fearful and started sucking her thumb. Sometimes, Tina accompanied her mom on trips to see Sandy. At these times, she was happy, totally interested and engrossed in the medical procedures given to her sister.

The stress on Lynda was dramatic. She lost twenty-five pounds in a matter of a month and was diagnosed with double pneumonia. Jerry couldn't seem to emotionally handle his family in crisis and buried himself in his work. The cancer treatment wreaked havoc on Sandy's small body. At this point Sandy was bald, weighed twenty-one pounds, and was in constant pain. She looked tiny and old. By the second week of October, after two blood transfusions, the doctors decided to take her off all cancer drugs. The medical team didn't think she would make it to Halloween. They gave her three weeks to live.

The news hit Lynda with a tsunami of hopelessness. Driving home from the hospital she found herself drowning in despair. On a California freeway she was sobbing so hysterically that tears blurred her vision. Afraid she would crash, she turned off the freeway onto an unfamiliar road. Almost immediately she spied a church shining in the October sun. She opened the door and entered. In front of her, a skylight over the altar radiated a powerful beam onto an open Bible. The lit passage told her not to lose faith. In her conversation with God she said, "If you let me keep her, I will tell her story. If she is to go, please let her go fast so she won't suffer." As she prayed, she visualized a pair of open hands. When she laid her precious daughter in those hands, a weight lifted, and for the first time in a long time she felt at peace. Her daughter's life was now in God's hands.

Lynda was finally able to talk to Sandy about death. It turned out Sandy's spirit had already figured it out. "I may go to heaven like my Nan. Don't worry, Mommy. If I die, Jesus and Nan will take care of me until you come." Sandy's purity of faith was something to behold.

The next six weeks were a blur. Lynda asked the Episcopal priest who helped after her mom's death to lay hands on Sandy. By the middle of November, the tumor in Sandy's liver had shrunk by half. Sandy was put on a mild chemotherapy drug to shrink the tumor further. By the end of November, Sandy's skeptical doctor, to Lynda's and Tina's delight, came running through the hospital cafeteria screaming, "The cancer is gone. It's gone! It's a miracle." Linda was in a state of grace.

Is this a fairytale where everyone lives happily ever after? No, this is real life, and Sandy's illness and miraculous recovery had an effect on every member of the family. They moved to Colorado to escape the crowds, drugs and smog of California. Children's Hospital in Denver helped and supported Sandy and her family as much as possible. There were, however, lasting effects of the cancer, radiation and chemotherapy. The doctors couldn't save Sandy's eye, she suffered from muscle weakness, and her growth was stunted. Years later she developed a seizure disorder.

Life was hard on Sandy. She was made fun of in school because of her looks. Despite the challenges, she played on a baseball team, was a Girl Scout, and participated in school activities. Throughout her life, she definitely has her down days, but the spirituality displayed at seven is ever present. Being an old soul, she cares about everyone. She has a special place in her big heart for the older generation like her Nan, and toddlers like her memory of three-year-old sister Tina.

Tina flourished. She was a high-school star, active in dance and poms. Because her interest in medicine as a toddler never waned, she received a double major in biology and chemistry in college. She then went on to medical school. She is now an intuitive, think-out-of-the-box doctor with a thriving practice. Her goal is to solve medical problems and save lives. She is married to a doctor. They have one daughter, who is in college and wants to go to medical school. Besides medicine, there is another carry-over from her three-year-old self. Her mother is perhaps the only one who notices the appearance of old fears and insecurities at stressful times.

Jerry was never able to emotionally deal with the family trauma and became an alcoholic. Lynda decided to join a codependency group in order to cope with his alcoholism. She learned how to set boundaries. She, with her girls, moved to their own place with the hope her action would be the impetus for Jerry's sobriety. Jerry divorced Lynda and married another woman. He continued to drink. Lynda was initially heartbroken but in time found being on her own, for the first time in her life, very freeing.

From her mother, Lynda inherited the brain chemistry

of depression. Her mother had showered love on Lynda and her siblings. She wouldn't consider suicide because she loved her children too much. Lynda learned from her mother that love was much stronger than depression. Her mother had given her a powerful tool to fight suicide. Even so, it was a fight. Many factors kept her from taking her own life—her faith, love of family and friends, and, like her mother, her absolute determination to never abandon her children. One day, a psychiatrist prescribed a new drug called Prozac. For the first time in her life, she didn't have to fight the heaviness and hopelessness of depression. She felt happy. Is this how normal people feel all the time, she wondered? The Prozac lasted for six joyous years and then stopped working.

Her relationship with God was complicated. After Sandy's recovery, Lynda felt both relief and fear. She was so grateful Sandy was alive, but she was pretty certain she didn't have the strength to go through another crisis of that magnitude. Because Sandy was spared, Lynda felt that every day she needed to prove her worth in God's eyes. If she didn't do life perfectly, God might decide to test her with another crisis she couldn't survive. Consciously, she knew she was getting her relationship with God mixed up with her relationship with her father. Her father was a perfectionist, judgmental Air Force officer. Growing up, Lynda felt she could never be good enough to get his approval. Her faith led her to seek therapy. The therapy technique most helpful to her self-esteem was called inner child work. Lynda, through a visualization process, was able to go back in time and see her child self. She pictured scared, three-year-old little Lynda hiding under a chair to escape her angry father. As an adult, she was able, using a soft, kind voice, to coax the child from her hiding place. As Lynda held her child self, a sense of safety, strength and peace filled her being. Her father was wrong; she was good enough! She was smart, capable and lovable. From that time on, she was able to give herself the love and acceptance her mother had given her, and that she had given to her children. She knew, with certainty, a loving, nonjudgmental God had led her to this insight.

For Lynda, all was well for many years. When she turned fifty, however, she found herself trying to weather a perfect storm. She was under an extreme amount of stress and definitely wasn't thinking clearly. Tina was married, and Sandy had bought and was living in her own townhouse. In her depression, she rationalized since her kids were doing fine, abandoning them was no longer a concern. She had an abusive boss, she came down with shingles, and to top it off a storm broke her favorite tree in the front yard. She told both her kids she was suicidal and checked herself into the hospital for a week.

The hospital had strict rules on what she could bring. She

couldn't believe they let her keep her hair dryer, when they took the tabs off of all the soft drinks. She put the hairdryer out of her mind, participated in group and individual therapy, and left the hospital with a new attitude wearing a string around her neck sporting a Coca-Cola tab. One can't take life too seriously.

Life improved. She quit her job and became a nanny for Tina and her husband. She watched her new little granddaughter Emma four days a week. Taking care of Emma was six years of bliss and reminiscent of her happy days with Tina and Sandy. When Emma went to school, Lynda worked in Tina's medical center. The combination of an effective anti-depressant, a great working environment and a peaceful home life has made Lynda's senior years fulfilling.

Today, retired seventy-five-year-old Lynda, fifty-five-year-old Sandy and Sandy's dog are happily living together. Sandy's self-absorbed but lovable Westy, named Tavish Duncan MacLeod, keeps life interesting. Lately, due to such a loving environment, even Tavish is considering others. The other day, Lynda had Tavish on her lap and was gently removing burrs from his fur. After she was done, she put him down. Immediately, he returned the favor by gently removing burrs from her clothing with his teeth.

Lynda starts her morning in prayer. Every day she prays for all children. She always gives a special thanks to God for her grown-up children Sandy and Tina and her granddaughter Emma.

COVID has been challenging for a busy extrovert like Lynda. To her credit, she has learned to sit in the sun on her porch and let her mind wander. She reminds herself that life is a gift, and she has the responsibility and privilege to live it to the fullest. She's convinced that happiness comes down to blessings, family, and the kindness of people around her. She laughs out loud, remembering the funny times. She says the serenity prayer many times a day because it keeps her centered. Spring, her favorite season, is just around the corner, and she will be buying seeds. She will nurture her seedling children and watch them grow. Lynda loves children.

When I asked her if I might write her story, she said she would think about it. In my mind's eye I pictured her pondering her decision on her porch. When she decided in the affirmative, she checked with both of her girls. "Yes Mom, do it!" was their enthusiastic answer. Forty-eight years ago, she promised God she would tell the miraculous story of Sandy and her family. She has told the story many times. She just hadn't visualized the story being in print in a book for and about seniors. She believes anything can happen in "our golden seasons," and it's all good!

16
My Life Designer

I had retired and was feeling anchorless and a little stuck when trying to navigate seniordom. I wished for an older, wiser person to show me the way. I wanted a mentor. Life was changing, but I wasn't. We had hired Mark, a general contractor, to complete our last and final remodel. Mark recommended we use a designer for the project, and he had just the right person in mind. At that time, I had no idea she was sent to me as a gift to re-design my life.

Into my world walked a breath of fresh air, a burst of new energy, an answer to my prayers. Her name was Pat. She was nine years older in age, and oh, so much younger in spirit and attitude. Her South African accent was lovely, her talent for design amazing, her interest in me and the project exciting and comforting.

Pat had retired many years before I met her. At the age of seventy-six she was willing to come out of retirement for her good friend and our general contractor, Mark. She had lived many places in the world and traveled extensively. This gave her an incredible amount of knowledge and insight into different cultures and beliefs. Pat was comfortable in her skin, and secure in her values and view of life. She lived her convictions without judging the opinions of others. She loved people, and people loved her.

She began mentoring me from the moment we met. My design acumen was sorely lacking. I had trouble visualizing space, thinking three dimensionally, and conceptualizing the finished product. She wasn't concerned. "All problems have a solution. The solution is usually a win-win. Sometimes the solutions are surprisingly simple." Because of changes in the kitchen, we were left with a view of some unsightly outlets. Her solution was to beautify the view and hide the outlets with a pitcher filled with fresh flowers.

Pat and I would go on trips together to hunt for the perfect flooring, appliances, fixtures and hardware. She had been out of the field for so long, many of her favorite places had gone out of business or moved. Because she relied on her memory and not Siri, more often than not we would find ourselves incredibly lost. There was one incident I remember clearly. It was almost 1:30 p.m., the place was in a sketchy part of Denver, and our purpose was to find the showroom Pat remembered as having great bathroom fixtures. Finally, after at least thirty minutes of wandering around, I called the phone number of the store, only to find they had moved several blocks away two years ago.

We were famished, but no worries—Pat remembered a great restaurant only a block away. The restaurant was nowhere to be found. How did Pat respond to this turn of events? She was amazed how Denver had changed, she laughed at her own ineptness, and was grateful for my patience and phone call. We ended up eating at a very good restaurant, while enjoying wonderful conversation and shopping at the amazing storeroom she remembered. Pat never felt lost because she found joy, humor, and beauty in every situation. Her vision and laughter were contagious.

Pat wanted to know about my life. She saw a photograph in our home and questioned me about it. I told her the photo represented my idyllic childhood; a scene of my siblings and me standing on a raft on Flathead Lake in Montana. Pat, an incredible artist, loved the happy innocence portrayed in the picture and decided to paint it. The painting captured my heart and childhood and means the world to me.

Pat was curious about my interests. I told her I liked to write and had authored my first book years ago. I confided to her I was in a slump. I hadn't written anything for a very long time. After reading my book, she said I had a gift and encouraged me to continue writing.

Pat was a wonderful cook, and she loved our kitchen. She laughed at my non-cook attitude. She suggested, when our project was finished, we should invite Mark, the contractor, and his family to the house for a brunch. She and Mark would cook. The project was completed, and the brunch happened. I provided the kitchen, utensils, orange juice, bacon and the dining room. Pat brought fresh flowers for the table and sour-cream-and-blueberry pancake batter. Mark and Pat prepared the delicious meal. The brunch was to be just a beginning. She thought we had a perfect party house and threatened to teach me how to make two easy hors d'oeuvres for guests. Sadly, the cooking class never happened.

Pat was my designer for only three short years. I am still spatially challenged, I do not cook or know how to make easy hors d'oeuvres, and I am not an artist. These are not the things she taught me. Instead, she re-designed my life by helping me get unstuck, changing my attitude, bringing joy, laughter and beauty back into my life. She gave me a sense of purpose and the energy and courage to develop my own talents.

Pat passed away on June 2, 2020, of a rapidly growing brain tumor. She was seventy-nine years old. Because of her beliefs, she chose not to prolong her life using chemo or radiation. The tumor affected her ability to speak, making it impossible to have a conversation by phone. I wanted to tell her how much she meant to me. I couldn't thank her or say goodbye in person because of the COVID pandemic. My only comfort is my belief Pat knew how I felt about her.

She lives in my mind; I am reminded of her every day. I

feel her presence in my home; Pat touched almost all our rooms through appliances, fixtures, arrangements, color and design.

Most of all, she lives in my heart. Her painting of my childhood brings me immense joy. My pitcher holding fresh flowers reminds me daily of the beauty and vision of her life.

I miss you, Pat. Thank you for redesigning my life and being my friend forever.

17
Reminiscing

As the sun sets on *Our Golden Seasons,* I am left with a warm glow in my heart. Writing this book, as a senior, for and about seniors has been immensely fulfilling. In trusting me to write their story, old and new friends gave me a precious gift. I am deeply honored. Trusting friends to critique my book was also a gift.

Although each life story is uniquely different in circumstance, their essence is the same. Displays of courage and resilience in overcoming obstacles is woven throughout the book. Grateful for all of life's lessons and viewing every challenge as an opportunity to learn and grow is also a common thread.

Writing about the antics of aging was easy and fun. Playing with words and definitions, delightful. Yukking it up with Yokes, always interesting and enjoyable.

My parents' stories gave me new insight, appreciation and empathy. Because of her dementia, Mom's story was the most difficult to write. In shining a bright light on memories of growing up with the wisest, most incredible and fun mom ever, thoughts of her dementia grew dim in comparison.

Our Golden Seasons filled my life with purpose. With a new focus on friends and family, reminiscing became my favorite pastime. For a senior-friendly mood changer, reminiscing is an uplifting and effective tool. When feeling down, often thoughts of younger years float through my mind. Memories flow back in time and pool together in one special place... Flathead Lake, Montana. At the "The Lake," my mind returns to feelings of love, joy and peace.

The Lake

Wondrous water runs through my years

Whispers of waves lap at my consciousness
And bubble up to the surface of my mind

Carefree days of the sun dancing
Spraying sparkles of light on ripples of water
The air is filled with squeals of delight

Exhilarating and electrically charged times
Powerful peaks and valleys of white caps
Standing strong, making waves
Pushing boundaries to the shore's edge

Sailing, splashing, skiing, swimming and smiling
Chatting, connecting, confiding and canoeing
Fishing, family and friends
Relaxing, rowing, rafting
Laughing, loving
Living

The lake fills my senses, like the feel of floating
Like the smell of willows and the taste of raspberries
Like the sound of waves and sight of moonlight shimmering on a
lake of glass

Reminiscing
Reflecting pools of life's most precious moments

Giving courage to ride the waves of aging

18
Bird's Words and Phrases
First and Only Senior Collegiate Dictionary

A

A long stretch: a senior touching toes while keeping knees straight

A wrinkle in time: (1) minimizing of the wrinkle problem (2) a great children's book

Age-old: a description of a senior

Agitator: (1) itchy or irritating clothing (2) icky or irritating close relationships especially during a pandemic (3) washing machine part

Alignment: a medical professional's wish for a senior's skeletal structure

B

Back down: excruciating back pain, unable to walk, down for the count

Back in: (1) back has been adjusted and is in alignment (2) a senior parking challenge

Back in circulation: (1) the circulatory system of the body is working (2) dating again at a late stage in life

Back out: (1) back is out of alignment (2) another senior parking challenge

Back up: on your feet again after injury or illness

Blanket statement: (1) overgeneralization such as "all seniors are cranky and crotchety" (2) description of a cozy comforter

BLT: (1) an acronym used by medical staff meaning no bending, lifting, or twisting after surgery (2) a sandwich

Brace yourself: accumulating assorted devices for support of various body parts

Brain drain: (1) smart seniors leaving the workforce (2) any attempt at intellectual reasoning after 5 pm (3) a surgically placed shunt to drain fluid

Break-in: (1) internal fracture (2) getting used to new hearing aids, orthotics, smart phones

Breakout: (1) escape from a nursing home (2) a rash, shingles

Breathless: (1) a need for oxygen or APAP, BiPAP, CPAP (2) witnessing nature at its best (3) excitement of watching achievements and celebrations of family and friends

C

Cane and able: use of a cane to be able to walk

Caught flat-footed: needing orthotics

Charmed: owner of a charm bracelet

Chin-up: (1) plastic surgery to tighten up saggy chin (2) an exercise performed in younger years

Climate change: (1) hot flashes, night sweats (2) trouble regulating body temperature

Confirm: (1) not strict, inclined to be wishy-washy (2) against body firmness requiring more than an hour of exercise every day

Confusion: against fusion of the neck or back

Contented: (1) a person who no longer wishes to tent-camp (2) a happy camper

Context: against texting, emailing, or any computer-generated communication, preferring old-fashioned face-to-face communication. Letter writing and phone calls are also acceptable.

Core issue: a weakening of the body core

Cover story: (1) talking about bedspreads, comforters and quilts (2) wearing loose and comfy clothing during a pandemic

Cursive: (1) old-fashioned handwriting (2) a person who tends to curse

D

Download: (1) what gravity does to a senior's body (2) loading down your kids or grandkids with questions about the internet

Downsize: (1) losing height with age (2) losing weight

F

FaceTime: (1) as females age, they need more time to fix their face (2) time to face reality of how one looks on Zoom

Fiber optics: looking at a bottle of Citrucel

Framework: (1) skeletal structure (2) work done on body frame by medical professionals

Fuzzy thinking: (1) focusing on items made out of soft materials such as blankets, slippers, pajamas (2) senior memories that distort facts

G

Getting traction: pulling on a limb or muscle

Going viral: (1) a case of COVID-19, the flu, a cold (2) 40,000 to 100,000 hits on the Internet, whatever that means

Good to go: state of condition after bladder surgery

Gray matter: (1) deciding whether to dye hair (2) an issue not involving black and white thinking (3) color of surroundings before cataract surgery

Gravity of the situation: sagging body parts

Gut feeling: (1) stomach issues (2) response to spicy foods

H

Hardware: an older woman wearing high heels

Handicap: grabbing any hat handy for sun protection

Hardbody: hard of hearing, hard of seeing, hardened arteries (as read on a greeting card)

Heart-felt: (1) precursor to a heart attack (2) panic attack

Heated discussion: (1) a discussion of heat options to alleviate pain (2) conversation concerning temperature settings at home

Home runs: staying in place just in case

Hope chest: use of implants, good bras, bralettes to provide hope against depressing and sagging tissues

Housekeeper: doing everything physically and financially possible to stay living in the home

I

Ice Age: time of life when you need to use ice packs after many physical activities to reduce swelling

I'm screwed: a recipient of surgeries using screws

I'm stoned: a recipient of a massage using hot stones

Inflammatory remarks: discussion of inflammation in the body

I've got your back: reassuring comments from back specialists, PTs, massage therapists (as read on a wooden plaque)

J

Joint accounts: (1) discussion about the joints in the body (2) talk about experiences with smoking pot (without inhaling?)

M

Masking emotions: hiding frustration about not being able to hear, breathe, and see facial expressions during a pandemic

Memory bank: (1) remembering the location of the bank (2) banking memories without using a password-protected smart vault

O

On my nerves: (1) a cyst, bulging disc, tumor, or anything touching a nerve and causing pain (2) too much together time during COVID-19

P

Pain in the butt or neck: actual physical pain experienced in the body

Pedal pushers: (1) aggressive florists (2) an old-fashioned word for Capris (3) riders on adult tricycles with big baskets for groceries

Preamble: (1) a senior preparing to go for a walk (2) reminiscing about youthful romping, running, jumping, and skipping

Precursor: recalling years when swearing was discouraged or wasn't allowed

Profusion: agreeing to surgery for fusing certain body parts

Promotion: a senior wanting to stay active

R

Rash statement: talk of skin issues and tissues

Reformed: (1) no longer engaged in the risky behaviors of one's youth; using SPF 30+ instead of baby oil when tanning, not partying as much, drinking more water, cutting down on junk food, refusing to leap over high fences in a single bound (you get the idea) (2) any medical or dental procedure that changes the form of the body

Replacement cost: (1) the medical cost of do-overs (2) any transplant procedure

Restroom: (1) a room a senior may visit in order to take a nap (2) a facility where location and availability are extremely important

Retired: discussion about being tired

Retraction: discussion about being stretched to the limit

Retreats: discussion about desserts, good restaurants, vacations, hanging out with family

Rock 'n' roll: (1) a rocking chair and a walker (2) great music

S

Seniority: (1) older and wiser (2) a senior sorority

Skeleton crew: a group of medical professionals who work on the skeletal structure of the body

Social Security: an organization or group of friends who help a person feel secure

Socket wrench: an accident or activity that dislocates a bone

Software: (1) comfortable clothing and slippers (2) blankets, comforters, fluffy towels

Spur of the moment: a bone spur currently causing pain

Steeled: steel put in the body that may set off metal detectors

Stepping up to the plate: ready to eat at mealtime

Straight man: (1) someone who has good posture (2) someone who has had a successful back surgery (3) a comedian's sidekick, like Gracie Allen was to George Burns

Stretch of the imagination: a senior doing the splits

Stroke of luck: a stroke causing minimal brain damage

Swell: (1) inflamed body parts (2) the old-fashioned word "swell" meant good

T

Take a break: (1) the breaking of a bone (2) toes up

Thin skinned: skin prone to cuts and bruises

Time crunch: senior taking time to chew food

Thongs: (1) a senior's word for flip-flops (2) skimpy underwear

Trash talk: deciding who will take out the trash

Tough pill to swallow: older people who have a tough time swallowing big pills

U

Uplifting: (1) plastic surgery (2) straps or pulleys used in exercise (3) certain bras

Using your noodle: use of a Styrofoam tube in a pool to help a person stay afloat while exercising

W

Wrinkle free: a false hope after plastic surgery

Y

Young in spirit: a senior

Acknowledgments

I am so grateful to my husband Yokes for his constant support and for providing an endless supply of funny senior stories. He is my companion, my love and my best friend.

Thank you to all the incredibly resilient seniors, past and present, who contributed their stories to this book.

A special thanks to Clare Alsko for the hours of valuable feedback and perspective. Her kind, thoughtful and literate responses helped make this writing project fun and enjoyable.

A shout out to super seniors Diann Kissell, Pat Starker, Janice Bede and Mary Michele Beaty who read the entire text and provided their unique critique. There are so many more people (you know who you are) who provided support and encouragement throughout this project. My children and entire extended family are a joy. Most have no idea what it means to be a senior, but they will eventually learn.

I am so very thankful for Katriena Knights' editorial expertise. She is young enough to know her way around a computer, and old enough to be patient with this computer illiterate author. Much gratitude to my talented and tolerant son Chris for designing the front and back covers. Thank you to Kayla

Niksic for saving the day with her formatting skills.

I would be remiss if I didn't mention my family of origin. My parents gave me such a safe and rich environment in which to learn and grow. My sister Leslie has been there for me through all my writing endeavors. She is honest with her feedback. She definitely thinks I went overboard with the puns in this project. My brother Brad came to my rescue in my early writing days by providing some invaluable tips on how to tell a story. At present, however, he is against the senior subject and all that it implies. Finally, I am thankful for the time I had with my sister Susan and sad she will never experience senior life.